CRAZY MAZEY

UNICORN MAZES

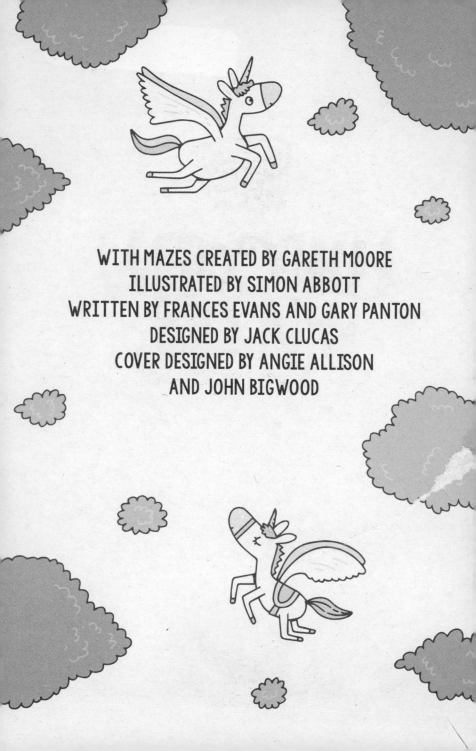

WITH MAZES CREATED BY GARETH MOORE
ILLUSTRATED BY SIMON ABBOTT
WRITTEN BY FRANCES EVANS AND GARY PANTON
DESIGNED BY JACK CLUCAS
COVER DESIGNED BY ANGIE ALLISON
AND JOHN BIGWOOD

CRAZY MAZEY

UNICORN MAZES

Buster Books

First published in Great Britain in 2019 by Buster Books,
an imprint of Michael O'Mara Books Limited,
9 Lion Yard, Tremadoc Road, London SW4 7NQ

 www.mombooks.com/buster   Buster Books @BusterBooks

Mazes 22, 44, 48, 57, 83 and 85 © Gareth Moore 2019
All other mazes, illustrations and layouts © Buster Books 2019

A CIP catalogue record for this book is available
from the British Library.

ISBN: 978-1-78055-667-3

2 4 6 8 10 9 7 5 3 1

Papers used by Buster Books are natural, recyclable products made
from wood grown in sustainable forests. The manufacturing processes
conform to the environmental regulations of the country of origin.

Printed and bound in October 2019 by CPI Group (UK) Ltd,
108 Beddington Lane, Croydon, CR0 4YY, United Kingdom

MIX
Paper from
responsible sources
FSC® C020471

CONTENTS

ARE YOU A-MAZE-ING?

Mazes come in all shapes and sizes. In this book, some mazes are circular, some are square and some even come in unicorn shapes, but all of them are sprinkled with magic.

The mazes get tougher as you progress through the levels, starting with Bronze Unicorns and working up to Silver and Gold Unicorns. The final level is Diamond Unicorns, conquered only by the true maze masters. But don't worry – you're about to become one!

Look out for the arrows that show you where to start and finish each puzzle. With some mazes, you need to dodge obstacles blocking your way. With others, there are items you need to pass by or collect as you complete them.

Along the way, you can learn all kinds of fantastic facts about unicorns and their magical friends.

Best of luck and have fun!

LEVEL ONE:
BRONZE UNICORNS

MAZE 1

Make your way through
this unicorn silhouette.

MAZE 2

MAZE 3

Guide this unicorn to the flower meadow. Avoid the dragons – you don't want to wake them up!

MAZE 4

Can you take the bee to the middle of the magical flower?

DID YOU KNOW?

It's hard to spot a unicorn, which is why many people believe they only exist in fairy tales. But you just need to know where to look and how to find them.

Different types of unicorns have different magical powers, which also make them harder to see. Some unicorns have manes that can make them invisible, while others can fly.

In Unicornland, unicorns live alongside lots of other magical beings, from dragons, gnomes and fairies to llamacorns, mermicorns and kittycorns. You'll encounter many of these creatures as you work your way through the mazes in this book.

MAZE 5

Can you get from one side of this maze to the other,
and meet the unicorn in the middle on your way?

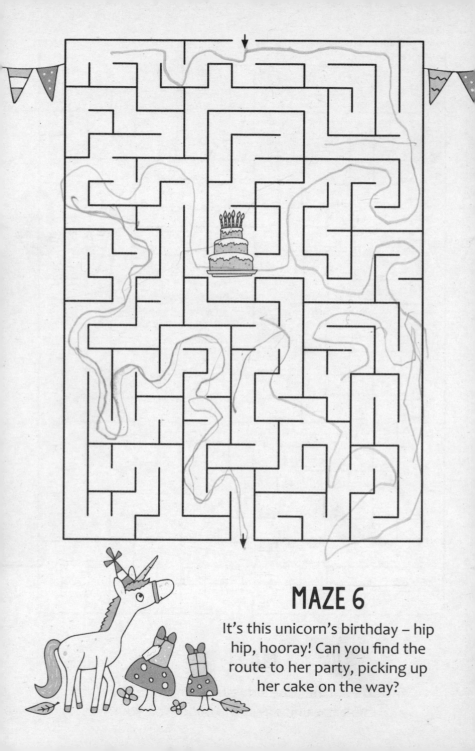

MAZE 6

It's this unicorn's birthday – hip hip, hooray! Can you find the route to her party, picking up her cake on the way?

MAZE 7

Now can you eat your way through
the birthday cake, from top to bottom?

MAZE 8

Guide this unicorn back home through the swamp, avoiding the ogres and other things blocking the paths.

MAZE 9

Can you cross the bridge
without disturbing the troll?

DID YOU KNOW?

The first unicorns to exist were called the
Golden Unicorn and the Silver Unicorn.

The Golden Unicorn and the Silver Unicorn were
born as horses but were transformed into unicorns
when they ran through a magical waterfall.

The Golden and Silver Unicorns are the
ancestors of all unicorns. It is said that when
they touched their horns to the ground, a new
family of unicorns would spring from that spot.

A group of unicorns is called a blessing.
A baby unicorn is called a youngling.

MAZE 10

Can you find the way to
this unicorn's treehouse?

MAZE 11

This unicorn has offered to take the
king out for the day in his carriage.
Can you solve the maze?

MAZE 12

Now can you reach the king in the
middle of the carriage maze?

MAZE 13

Find the route through the
most magical tree in the forest.

MAZE 14

DID YOU KNOW?

Each and every unicorn is filled with magic,
from the top of its horn to the tip of its tail.

Unicorns with wings are incredibly rare.
They are known as pegacorns, in reference
to a mythological flying horse called Pegasus.

Not all flying unicorns have wings. A family of unicorns
known as 'Desert Flames' use magical powers in their
hooves to help them take to the skies. Their hooves
glow orange when they are ready to take flight,
and they run at great speeds before lifting off.

Desert Flame unicorns are caring animals
and will always help people who need them.

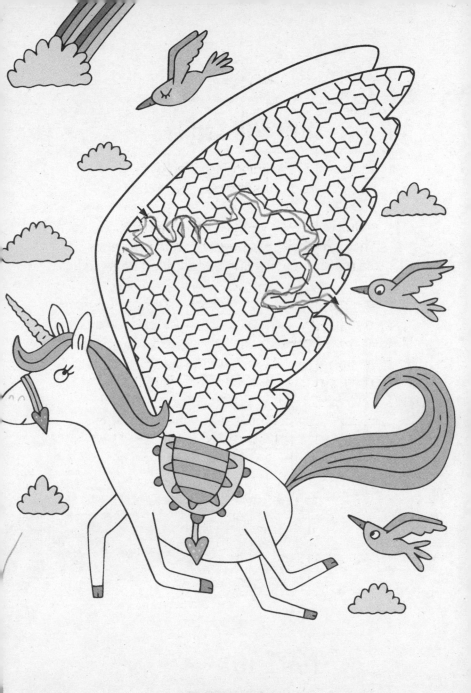

MAZE 15

MAZE 16

Munch your way through this
hungry unicorn's ice lolly.

MAZE 17

MAZE 18

Can you get to the middle of this moon maze?

LEVEL TWO:

SILVER UNICORNS

MAZE 19

Take this crab through the underwater maze, meeting his mermicorn friend along the way. Avoid the jellyfish.

MAZE 20

MAZE 21

MAZE 22

This brave knight is off to battle the dragon. Help him find his way to its lair.

DID YOU KNOW?

Unicorn poo is rainbow-coloured.
It smells like a mix of honeysuckle,
raspberries and freshly mown grass.

❀

A unicorn's diet depends on its habitat.
Unicorns that live in cold climates will search for
moss underneath the snow. Unicorns that live
in deserts are especially fond of cactus plants.

❀

Unicorns like to drink from the crystal-clear
waters of mountain springs. They will also lick
the morning dew from roses and buttercups.

MAZE 23

Find your way through
the unicorn poo.

MAZE 24

Guide this unicorn safely
through the thunderstorm.

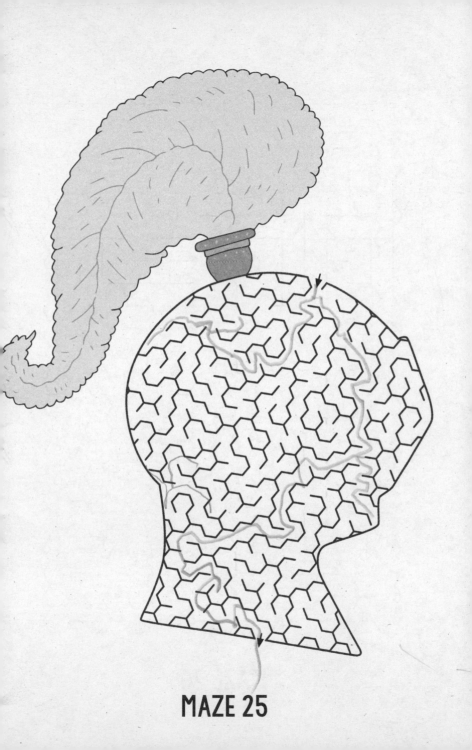

MAZE 25

MAZE 26

MAZE 27

DID YOU KNOW?

Look up into the night sky and you will
see that unicorns are in the stars.

They're represented as a collection of stars
called Monoceros, which means 'unicorn' in Greek.

Monoceros is hard to see with the naked eye,
but if you look with a telescope you'll find it.

Some unicorns, known as Water Moons, can only
be seen on clear nights when they are illuminated
by the light of the Moon and the stars.

MAZE 28

MAZE 29

MAZE 30

This enchanted butterfly has a maze on both wings. Can you make it from one wing to the other? When you reach the arrow at the bottom of the top wing, you can jump across to the arrow on the lower wing.

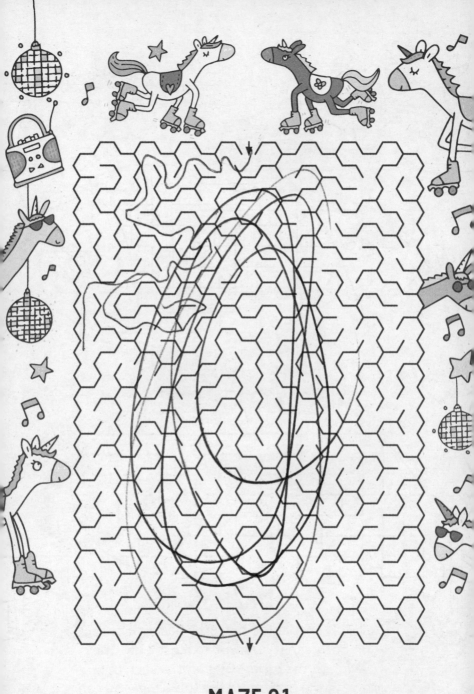

MAZE 31

MAZE 32

Find a way down this waterfall.

DID YOU KNOW?

Some unicorns love the cold. Unicorns called
Ice Wanderers live wherever it is snowy. They have
white coats and cream-coloured manes and tails
to help them blend in with their surroundings.

⊗

The next time it snows, keep an eye
out for Ice Wanderer footprints. Their
hooves leave a snowflake shape.

⊗

Ice Wanderers send messages to one another
by shooting brightly coloured lights into the
sky from their horns. Some people call these
displays the Northern and Southern lights.

⊗

Ice Wanderers that live in the north have
horns made of ice, while those that live
in the south have horns of pearl.

MAZE 33

It's getting cold outside! Can you guide this unicorn to her woolly winter hat?

MAZE 34

Can you guide the kittycorn and
the puppycorn to the tasty cake?

MAZE 35

MAZE 36

MAZE 37

Find your way through the maze, meeting
the unicorn in the middle as you go.

MAZE 38

MAZE 39

Can you reach the middle of the hot-air balloon?

DID YOU KNOW?

Some unicorns can control the weather. They can create lightning, change the course of a rain cloud and spread sunshine.

The unicorns that are most in-tune with the weather are known as Storm Chaser unicorns. Legend has it that, long ago, there lived a blessing of four young Storm Chasers. Each one held a corner of the sky in its mouth and, together, they kept the sky in place.

❀

A thunderstorm is said to happen when a baby pegacorn grows its wings.

❀

Some people believe that if you see a rainbow, it means that your guardian unicorn is nearby.

MAZE 40

MAZE 41

Take the prince and princess
through the maze. They
want to say hello to the
unicorn on the way.

MAZE 42

MAZE 43

MAZE 44

Can you get from the top of this unicorn's maze to the bottom?

MAZE 45

MAZE 46

Help the unicorn find the best route back to his house,
avoiding the gnomes and stones blocking the paths.

DID YOU KNOW?

Unicorns have been depicted in books and art since ancient times. They even featured on old coins.

Although unicorns differ in their appearance and magical powers, they all share the same five qualities: magic, loyalty, grace, kindness and strength.

Unicorns are thought to live for hundreds of years.

The Great Library of Unicornland contains a vast collection of books about unicorns, as well as records of all the other magical animals and plants that inhabit the kingdom.

MAZE 47

MAZE 48

Can you reach the other side of this moon?

MAZE 49

Help this flying unicorn
make her way through
the starry night sky.

MAZE 50

These children and their unicorn friend are lost in the woods. Help them find their way out, avoiding the squirrels (they throw nuts!).

MAZE 51

MAZE 52

Make your way to the piggycorn in the
middle of this maze and out the other side.

LEVEL THREE:

GOLD UNICORNS

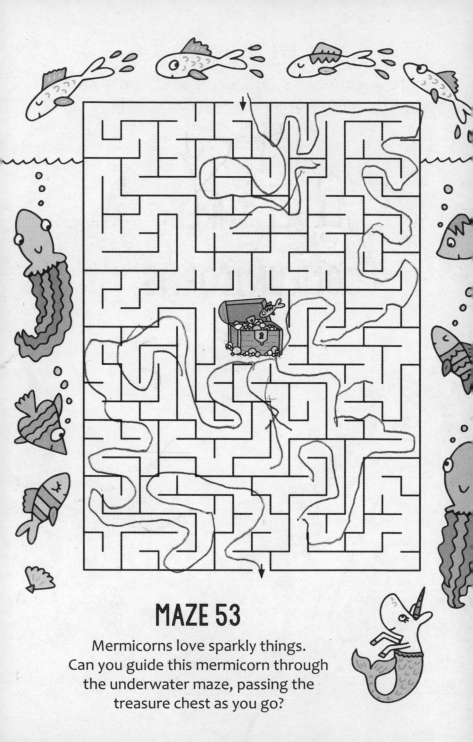

MAZE 53

Mermicorns love sparkly things.
Can you guide this mermicorn through
the underwater maze, passing the
treasure chest as you go?

MAZE 54

Find a way from the pirate's mouth to the end of his grizzly beard, avoiding the bits of his breakfast.

MAZE 55

These two unicorns want to get to
the ice cream van before it leaves.
Can you take them through
this maze to visit it?

MAZE 56

DID YOU KNOW?

Unicorns are active creatures and
spend most of their time outdoors.

❁

Some of their favourite pastimes include
cross-country running, tennis and volleyball.

❁

Young unicorns also love to play a
ring toss game with their horns.

❁

Mermicorns are particularly good at
synchronized swimming, while unicorns
who live in cold climates love to ice skate.

MAZE 57

This unicorn is late for his tennis lesson with the Big Bad Wolf. Help him find his way there.

MAZE 58

MAZE 59

MAZE 60

Find your way through the maze, making sure you
meet the pandacorn in the middle on your way.

MAZE 61

MAZE 62

MAZE 63

Can you help this trick-or-treating unicorn find a route to the house at the end of the maze? Avoid all the other houses.

DID YOU KNOW?

Unicorns can live in all sorts of places – from deep within the most magical forests to the mysterious, icy peaks of the tallest mountains.

Desert Flame unicorns live in arid and rocky landscapes. Their coats are sandy-brown and they have flame-coloured manes. Their bronze horns twist like the wind-swept desert sands.

❀

Desert Flame unicorns are protective herd animals and are renowned for helping people in distress.

❀

They are most active at midday, when the Sun is high and the air is hot.

MAZE 64

Guide the unicorn through the desert maze, avoiding the prickly cacti.

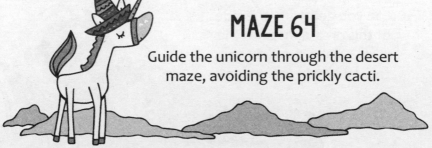

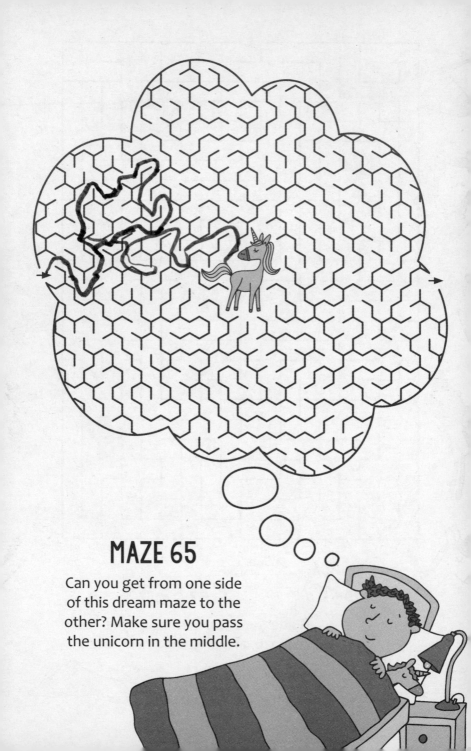

MAZE 65

Can you get from one side
of this dream maze to the
other? Make sure you pass
the unicorn in the middle.

MAZE 66

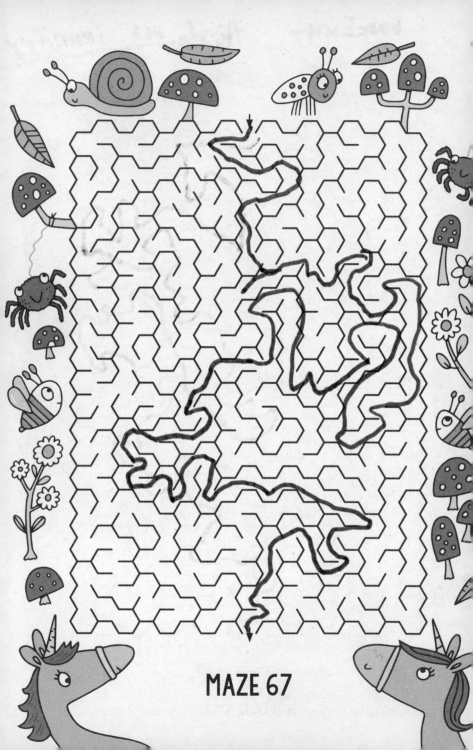

MAZE 67

MAZE 68

Make your way to the middle of the unicorn onesie.

DID YOU KNOW?

Unicorns' horns are made of precious
materials, such as coral, opal and silver.
Many unicorns have horns that glow.

❀

Different types of unicorns leave different hoof
prints. Woodland Flower unicorns, for instance,
have heart-shaped prints while Storm Chaser
unicorns have lightning-bolt prints.

❀

Unicorns are wise animals and each family passes
knowledge down through the generations.

❀

If you throw a perfectly round pebble into a
pond, you can make a wish on a unicorn.

MAZE 69

MAZE 70

This little horse has always wanted
to be a unicorn. Can you lead him
to the unicorn costume?

MAZE 72

Help this girl find her
lost unicorn toy and get
through the maze.

MAZE 73

MAZE 74

Help this bumblecorn make
his way through the maze,
taking a sip of nectar from
the flower on his way.

MAZE 75

DID YOU KNOW?

Unicorns have big appetites. Like horses,
grasses and hay form a big part of their diet.

They will also search for fruit such as
apples, cherries and wild strawberries.

Unicorns like to eat more unusual
berries, flowers and plants as well.
Some of their favourites include
bilberries, water lilies and orchids.

Every spring, unicorns travel to the Enchanted
Meadows. This is the only place in Unicornland
where a rare species of magical snowdrop grows.
Each unicorn eats just one flower to give their
powers a boost for the rest of the year.

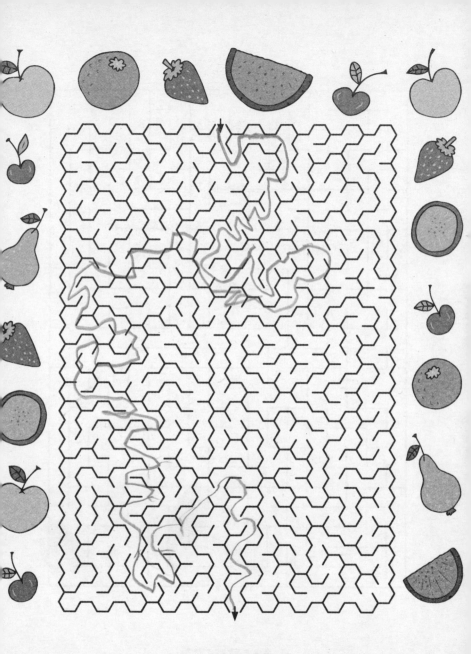

MAZE 76

MAZE 77

Try to reach the flamingocorn before
finding your way out of the maze.

MAZE 78

MAZE 79

Mrs Deer has a new fawn.
Can you help the unicorn visit her?

LEVEL FOUR:

DIAMOND UNICORNS

MAZE 80

Can you conquer the mazes on these tall buildings?

MAZE 81

MAZE 82

MAZE 83

DID YOU KNOW?

The fields and forests of Unicornland are filled
with enchanted, sweet-smelling flowers.

⚘

They provide a home for magical insects,
such as bumblecorns and buttercorns.

⚘

A bumblecorn's horn glows yellow
when it gets close to nectar. Like regular
bumblebees, bumblecorns are particularly
keen on lavender, heather and foxgloves.

⚘

The patterns on a buttercorn's wings change
depending on its mood. Some rare species
of buttercorn have heart-shaped wings.

MAZE 84

Collect each apple on your way round the orchard. Be careful not to disturb the troll.

MAZE 85

Can you get to the middle
of the maze in the rainbow?

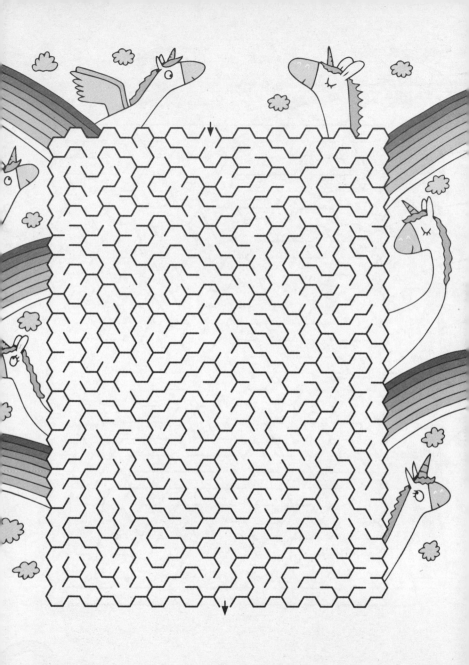

MAZE 86

MAZE 87

MAZE 88

Guide this unicorn through the snow, being careful to avoid the snowball-throwing snowmen.

DID YOU KNOW?

Mermicorns live in sea caves and coral palaces in unexplored parts of the oceans. Their horns are made from pearl or coral.

Mermicorns love to play in sea grass meadows and kelp forests with dolphicorns. They are sometimes seen swimming alongside sailors' boats.

Jellycorns are usually only seen on clear nights. They glow rainbow colours in the light of the moon.

Mermicorns love collecting sea pearls and rare shells. Pirates have been known to try to steal these treasures, but they are not usually successful because Mermicorns have very sharp horns!

MAZE 89

MAZE 90

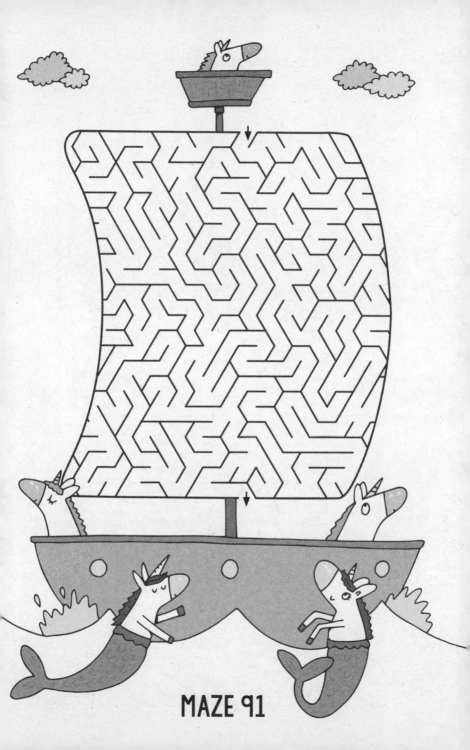

MAZE 91

MAZE 92

MAZE 93

Can you reach the llamacorn on
your way through the maze?

MAZE 94

MAZE 95

This unicorn is visiting her rabbit friend, but doesn't want to get lost in her maze of tunnels. Can you help?

DID YOU KNOW?

Kittycorns are meow-gical beings.
Cute and inquisitive, they are
always getting up to mischief.

Puppycorns are gentle, playful creatures.
They come in all shapes and sizes, from
tiny Chihuahuacorns to fluffy poodlecorns.

Pandacorns are extremely rare creatures
who live in remote cloud forests. They use their
black-and-white horns to cut down bamboo.

Llamacorns are lively, fun-loving animals. Their
woolly coats are usually lilac or pale pink. Clothes
made from llamacorn wool are said to make
the wearer especially good at dancing.

MAZE 96

MAZE 97

MAZE 98

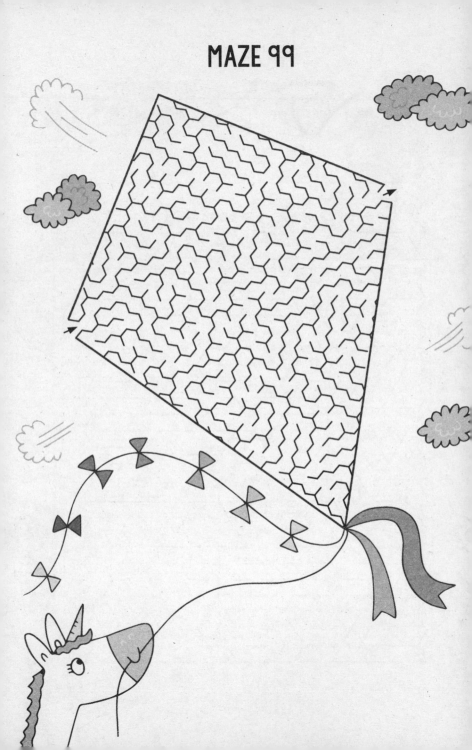

MAZE 100

MAZE 101

MAZE 102

Can you find a way through the maze?
Avoid the dinocorn in the middle.

DID YOU KNOW?

Dinocorns live in some of the most remote, mysterious parts of Unicornland. They have multi-coloured scales that change colour to match their surroundings. This means that, in spite of their size, they're hard to spot!

❀

Ogres are some of the laziest monsters in Unicornland. They live in rocky wastelands where there isn't much magic. A unicorn would make a tasty snack for an ogre, so they stay well away from them.

❀

The gnomes of Unicornland spend most of their time in underground caves. They are very greedy and love collecting gemstones.

MAZE 103

MAZE 104

Fly through this
rainbow maze.

MAZE 105

MAZE 106

This king has the biggest crown in all the land.
It even has room for a maze on it.

DID YOU KNOW?

A shooting star is actually a unicorn flying
between this world and Unicornland.

⚘

A solar eclipse heightens
a unicorn's magical powers.

⚘

Shadow Nights are the most mysterious
unicorns of all. They move between our
world and the world of dreams.

⚘

In unicorn lore, the Golden Unicorn
is said to represent the sun while the
Silver Unicorn represents the moon.

MAZE 108

Can you get to the other
side of this planet?

MAZE 109

Can you help the unicorns climb down
these magical mountain mazes?

MAZE 110

MAZE 111

It's been a long day, and this
unicorn is super sleepy.
Help her get to bed for
a well-earned rest.

ANSWERS

LEVEL ONE:
BRONZE UNICORNS

MAZE 3

MAZE 1

MAZE 4

MAZE 2

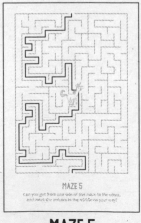

MAZE 5

MAZE 6

It's this unicorn's birthday - hip
hip, hooray! Can you find the
route to her party, picking up
her cake on the way?

MAZE 9

Can you cross the bridge
without disturbing the troll?

MAZE 7

Now can you eat your way through
the birthday cake, from top to bottom?

MAZE 10

Can you find the way
to the unicorn's treehouse?

MAZE 8

Guide this unicorn back home through
the swamp, avoiding the lights and
other things blocking the path.

MAZE 11

MAZE 14

MAZE 12

MAZE 15

MAZE 13

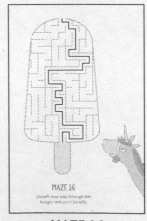

MAZE 16

MAZE 17

MAZE 19

MAZE 18

MAZE 20

LEVEL TWO:
SILVER UNICORNS

MAZE 21

MAZE 22

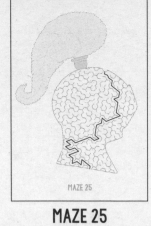

MAZE 25

MAZE 23

MAZE 26

MAZE 24

MAZE 27

MAZE 28

MAZE 31

MAZE 29

MAZE 32

MAZE 30

MAZE 33

MAZE 34

MAZE 37

MAZE 35

MAZE 35

MAZE 38

MAZE 38

MAZE 36

MAZE 36

MAZE 39

MAZE 40

MAZE 43

MAZE 41

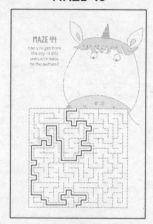

MAZE 44

MAZE 42

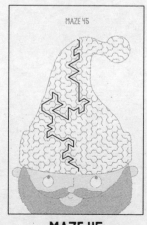

MAZE 45

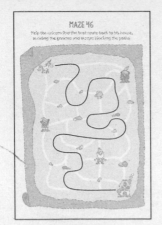

MAZE 46

MAZE 49

MAZE 47

MAZE 50

MAZE 48

MAZE 51

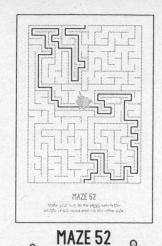

MAZE 52

Make your way to the peggy corn in the middle of this maze and out the other side.

MAZE 52

LEVEL THREE: GOLD UNICORNS

MAZE 54

Find a way from the pirate's mouth to the end of his grizzly beard, avoiding the bits of his breakfast.

MAZE 54

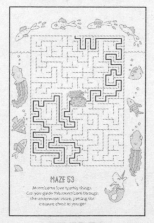

MAZE 53

Merunicorns love sparkly things. Can you guide this merunicorn through the underwater maze, picking the treasure chest as you go?

MAZE 53

MAZE 55

These two unicorns want to get to the ice cream van before it leaves. Can you take them through this maze so visit it?

MAZE 55

MAZE 56

MAZE 59

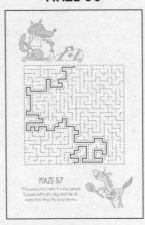

MAZE 57

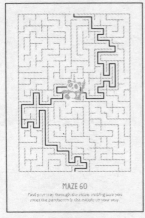

MAZE 60

MAZE 58

MAZE 61

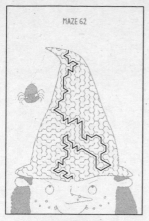

MAZE 62

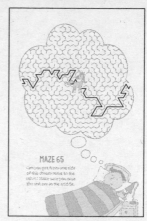

MAZE 65

MAZE 63

MAZE 66

MAZE 66

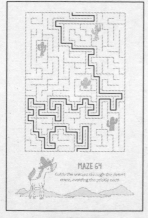

MAZE 64

MAZE 67

MAZE 67

MAZE 68

MAZE 71

MAZE 69

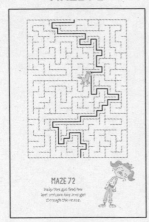

MAZE 72

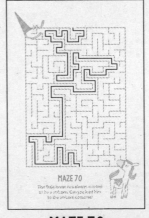

MAZE 70

MAZE 73

MAZE 74

MAZE 77

MAZE 75

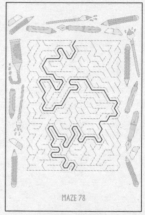

MAZE 78

MAZE 76

MAZE 79

LEVEL FOUR: DIAMOND UNICORNS

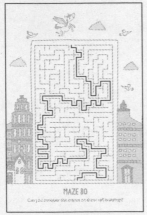

MAZE 80

MAZE 82

MAZE 81

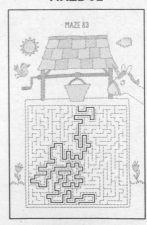

MAZE 83

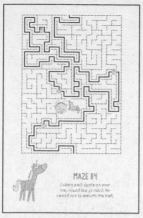

MAZE 84

MAZE 87

MAZE 85

MAZE 88

MAZE 86

MAZE 89

MAZE 90

MAZE 93

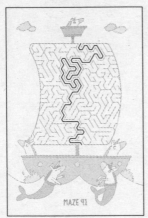

MAZE 91

MAZE 94

MAZE 92

MAZE 95

MAZE 96

MAZE 99

MAZE 97

MAZE 100

MAZE 98

MAZE 101

MAZE 102

MAZE 105

MAZE 103

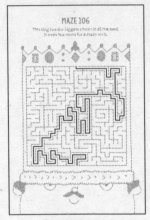

MAZE 106

MAZE 104

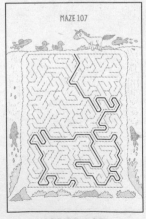

MAZE 107

MAZE 108

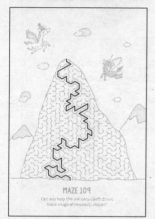

MAZE 109

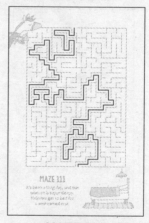

MAZE 111

MAZE 110

MORE CRAZY MAZES ...

ISBN: 978-1-78055-666-6